A Pocket Book *of* Confidence

15 Steps to Build Your Confidence
& Feel Like a Million Dollars!

TERESA BULFORD-COOPER

Copyright © 2020 by Teresa Bulford-Cooper.
All rights reserved.

This book or any portion thereof may not be reproduced or used in any manner whatsoever without the express written permission of the publisher except for the use of brief quotations in a book review.

Strenuous attempts have been made to credit all copyrighted materials used in this book. All such materials and trademarks, which are referenced in this book, are the full property of their respective copyright owners. Every effort has been made to obtain copyright permission for material quoted in this book. Any omissions will be rectified in future editions.

Cover and book design by: SWATT Books Ltd

Printed in the United Kingdom
First Printing, 2020

ISBN: 978-0-9926180-5-6

Teresa Bulford-Cooper
Crediton, Devon
EX17 5BW

www.teresabulfordcooper.com

Lack of confidence can be crushing and stand in the way of your emotional and physical freedom especially if you have been through a relationship breakdown, such as separation or divorce, it can knock your confidence and smash your self-esteem. So the thing to do is be brave and do something about it. If you always do what you've always done you always get what you've always got; in other words, something needs to change for you to move forward.

Following are 15 tips and short exercises to help you along your way to becoming that happy, confident lady you long to be – let her out so that you can feel like a million dollars!

1. What Are You Telling Yourself?

The first, and most important, thing to do is check in on your self-talk and listen to what it's saying. Is it telling you positive things about yourself, or is it negative jibber-jabber? If it's the negative voice, you need to dispel those thoughts and turn them into positive affirmations.

E.g. "I can't do it" into "I can do it".

The more you tell yourself you can do something, the more it will condition your mind to believe it – think it, and you can be it.

If you are like some ladies who can't seem to switch it off, try reasoning with yourself. Ask yourself why you are thinking these negative thoughts; question them.

If you are continuously putting yourself down or making jokes about the way you look; you need to stop it and start talking about yourself nicely – you wouldn't say it to your best friend so why say it to yourself?

You become what you tell yourself, so be kind and talk positively to yourself.

Exercise 1

Check-in with yourself throughout the day and take a minute to close your eyes and listen to what your inner voice is saying. What is it telling you? Become aware of negative thoughts and turn them into positive ones. Write some negative thoughts you have below and change them into positive ones.

Negative	Positive

2. Visual Keys

When you look in the mirror say something complimentary to yourself like, "hey, still got it, kid." Pick out things that you like and feel good about them. Accept those things that niggle you and remind yourself that we are not all perfect no matter who we are.

Pamper yourself and set yourself a spa time once a month (or two) and indulge in a pamper session to feel good about yourself.

Make a monthly date to get your nails done professionally – there's nothing like pretty nails to show off your feminine side.

Take a visit to the hairdresser and maybe change your hairstyle – a few highlights perhaps?

To make sure you look (which will also make you feel) at your best, make an appointment to see a stylist, (I use a lady from the company Colour Me Beautiful). They will advise on hairstyles, makeup, clothes, jewellery, shoes and your best colours. Worth every penny (I made lots of mistakes and spent a fortune over the years on wrong styles!)

Exercise 2

Look in the mirror and pick three good things about yourself each day. List them below.

Monday

_____
_____
_____

Friday

_____
_____
_____

Tuesday

_____
_____
_____

Saturday

_____
_____
_____

Wednesday

_____
_____
_____

Sunday

_____
_____
_____

Thursday

_____
_____
_____

3. Acknowledge Your Achievements

When was the last time you acknowledged the achievements you have made over the years? I encourage you to do that now – sit down with a pen and paper and make a list. It doesn't matter how big or small – they all count! Personally, I count getting out of bed in the morning as a huge achievement!

My achievements so far are:

_____
_____
_____
_____
_____
_____
_____

Following on from that, what about all the lovely things about you? Yes, we all have them so list them down. Firstly, all your physical attributes (yes you do have them even if it's just a small thing like eyelashes) and secondly all your values such as kindness, generosity etc.

No doubt you would pick out these things about someone else and say how much you admire them – you need to tell that to yourself too.

Keep a diary and write down at least 3 things you have done in the day that you are proud of. It can be little things as they are just as important as bigger things. Tell yourself well done and reflect on how good that makes you feel.

Talking of diaries, each evening make a note of 3 things you feel gratitude towards that happened in your day. Also, make a list of what you intend to do the next day.

Yes, I love lists! Lists keep you on track and make you accountable, it's too easy not to bother and watch daytime TV all day leaving you to feel unrewarded and underachieved by bedtime!

Exercise 3

Before you nod off to sleep at night think about those positive things you have achieved throughout the day and jot them down here.

4. Notice Your Posture and Stand Tall

Adopting a good posture not only makes you feel more confident but also makes you look it. If you notice how really confident people stand, you will notice that they stand up straight, shoulders back, head up, chin out slightly.

Try this for yourself and remember to look forward not down; positive confidant people always look ahead or up. Relax and remember to breathe! If you struggle with your posture you could try Pilates or Yoga classes to strengthen your core muscles.

Having a good posture will also ensure you are breathing at your optimum levels which will keep you alert. People are also magically drawn to those who have a good posture as they ooze confidence and likeability.

Exercise 4

To get an upright posture practice standing flat against a wall so that your head, bum and heels touch the wall and then walk forward or you can always do the old fashioned thing and practice walking with a book balancing on your head!

5. Set Yourself Some Goals

We all need direction in life, so setting goals is really important. It will give you a feeling of being in control, which will build your confidence.

Daily Goals
Set some small daily goals of what you want to achieve that day – this can be a few things or something you really need to get done.

Mid-Term Goals
Set a mid-term goal for about 5-6 months from now. What do you want to have achieved by then – see yourself there doing what it is you want to be happening.

My mid-term goal is:

_____

Long-Term Goals

Set a longer-term goal of 1-5 years or more. Where are you setting your sights to be then? Again imagine what you will be doing and who with.

My long-term goal is:

_____

It's important to write your goals down or they will remain a dream. By committing them to paper they become a reality. Every day do something towards achieving something towards each of them. Tick things off your list that you have accomplished to maximise those rewarding feelings.

Exercise 5

List your daily goals to keep on track. Tick them off as you achieve them.

6. Just Imagine That!

Use your imagination to visualize yourself being a positive person that you know or maybe someone you admire on TV. Become an actor and imagine stepping into your desired character, feel how that feels. See yourself as that confident positive person; notice the way she is standing and how she is holding herself. Notice the tonality of her voice and everything she is doing – things you want to be doing. This will help to program your brain into thinking that you have all the qualities from this person that you want.

Your brain does not know the difference between visualizing and actually having done something, so when you come to do whatever it is you have been visualizing your brain will think you have done it before.

Now practice by finding a quiet place where you can be undisturbed and just imagine yourself being in a positive situation that you need to be in. Maybe you are talking to someone or meeting someone for the first time. Notice how you are standing/sitting. Hear your voice, positive and confident, feel yourself being confident and in control.

See whatever it is you are doing going really well with a positive outcome.

When you get really good at this you can introduce a problem here and there and seeing yourself overcoming that problem with a positive outcome. The more you practice this the easier it will become. And remember to always be positive.

Exercise 6

Practice visualizing a few minutes a day – who you are stepping into and what attributes are you taking on board? Make a note of them and how that made you feel.

___

7. Educate Yourself

Take a course, (ideally with me!) in learning how to become that confident person. Most achievable things in life are all about having the confidence to do it. You can learn some really useful techniques to help you overcome your fears and find what's holding you back. Read up on self-confidence. The more you educate yourself about something, the less fear it will hold over you.

Many ladies have returned to adult education and started a whole new career, so it's never too late! If you think life has passed you by think again – your life skills are immeasurable and very sought after.

If you don't feel education is for you, how about doing a course on something that you enjoy? There are many things you could do, such as becoming a beauty therapist or a stylist. Have a look on Google for ideas and explore the options.

It's never too late to have a crack at starting up a small business – maybe you have a hobby that could turn into a small business? You may think OMG but believe me that although this will push you way out of your comfort zone it can be so rewarding, and your confidence will absolutely soar!

Exercise 7

Sit quietly for a few minutes and imagine you have a magic wand in your hand. When you wave it you can be anything or do anything you want – what would that be? Make a list of your results and take one action a day towards achieving it.

8. Get Out of Your Comfort Zone

Getting out of your comfort zone is essential. Be brave, take the plunge and try something new. Once you have achieved something you thought you could never do, no matter how big or small, it will start to increase your confidence. Why not join a club or a society?

Getting out and about and meeting new people will really help you gain confidence in so many ways. Think about your interests and explore some other local groups and societies to join. Have you thought about joining the University of the Third Age? This is open to anyone – you don't, despite the name, have to have gone to university. They have lots of subsections and lots of groups to join from walking, painting, history and science, to just meeting up for lunch once a month.

Is there a hobby or sport you enjoy or would like to try? Maybe there was something you used to do back in the day which you could revisit having let it slip by whilst looking after everyone else. My friend took up horse riding at 56, never having ridden a horse in her life but gave it a go.

She loved it and gained loads of new confidence from that experience.

Make sure you are getting plenty of exercise, especially outside, as this will enhance your mental state, letting loose those wonderful feel-good endorphins!

'Healthy body health mind' as the saying goes.

Exercise 8

Smile and speak to someone you don't know, maybe in the supermarket or hairdressers or wherever you may be – say hello and ask a question which could be about anything, e.g. I love your shoes where did you get them from? Is it going to rain all day? You get the idea. You will be amazed at the reaction you get back by just being friendly. Make a list of sentences you could come up with to start a conversation.

9. Get Your Finances in Order

Being in control of your financial position will give you a feeling of empowerment and confidence. Knowing exactly where you stand financially is a key factor in feeling confident about your future. So, make sure you are managing your finances correctly and planning for those future events. This will give you a clear vision of what's ahead and how to cope.

It may be that you need to find a financial advisor to help you with this. Don't be afraid of approaching some and just asking them a few questions – they are there to help you and can take the strain out of worrying about your assets. Importantly, you do not have to have vast revenue to take advantage of an advisor and it's just a phone call to see if they can help you.

Having financial guidance is really important if it's an area that you are uncertain about. If you have recently become divorced or acquired some additional revenue, now is very much the time to be seeking this.

If you do approach financial advisors, make sure you look at their credentials and have some conversations with them before you commit yourself.

Exercise 9

Set up an emergency savings fund for those rainy days to cover things you have not budged for. Put some money aside in it every week/month. Make a list of all the scenarios that you may not have thought about before. How much can you put aside for these should any of them happen?

_____
_____
_____
_____
_____
_____
_____
_____
_____
_____
_____
_____
_____
_____
_____
_____

10. Remove Negative People From Your Life and Stop Being a Doormat!

If you want to become confident (which I guess you do since you are reading this!) then you need to be around confident people; people who will build you up and always see the good things about everything. They will be constantly telling you how great you are and how good you are at things. Negative people are toxic and will constantly criticize you and drag you down, so get rid of them!

Learn to say "No". I bet you are always being asked to do favour's for others if you lack confidence. People lacking confidence tend to want to please others to gain self-gratification. We all love to be liked; however, it is important to realise the difference of being genuinely liked and being taken for granted, otherwise, you will be a doormat and forever be running around after other people getting nothing in return but worn out!

You can say no in nice ways, such as "I'm sorry, I am really busy. Could you ask someone else?" These people soon get fed up with asking you and will move onto someone else. They will think no less of you for saying no – in fact they may realise that you have a backbone and start treating you with the respect that they should, and that you deserve.

Exercise 10

List 3 ways that you can say "NO' in a nice way. Practice saying them out loud so that it becomes second nature.

___
___
___
___
___
___
___
___
___
___
___
___
___
___
___
___
___
___

11. Don't Compare

Constantly comparing yourself with other people is self-destroying and will ruin any confidence you have. Remember that we are all special in our own way and you should look for your own unique qualities within. Live by your own rules and don't fall in with everyone else because you want to feel accepted. Be the shepherd, not the sheep!

Watch out for social media – it can be a confidence killer. Spending time on Facebook, Instagram and other social media platforms can have a draining effect on your confidence.

Before you realise it, you are starting to feel that everyone else is having a much better life than you, that they are happier, have everything and are that confident person you are longing to be.

Well, I can tell you this is as far from the truth as it can be. Everyone likes to put the best side of the story on these sites to be popular or draw attention to themselves. Take it all with a pinch of salt and don't compare your life with theirs.

Exercise 11

Look at what's important and really matters to you. Make a list of those lovely things that people say about you (they are called your values). An example might be being kind, honest, loving, caring.

12. Sleep Hygiene

I cannot tell you how important it is to have a good night's sleep – ideally about eight hours, but we do seem to need less as we age. To be at your optimum you need to have a good sleep pattern in place as nothing zaps your energy faster than feeling worn out. To feel confident, you need to be on top form.

Set yourself a bedtime each night and stick to it. Get off any social media an hour before you go to bed as the blue light from your phone/computer will be telling your brain that it is time to wake up!

Start telling yourself that it's coming up to bedtime about an hour before bed so that your brain starts to wind down and prepare for sleep.

Try not to drink too much alcohol in the evening as this will wake you at about 3 am when your body is at its coolest and you will have problems getting back to sleep.

Cut back on other stimulants, such as caffeine, as they will also keep you awake.

For more on sleep pop me an email and I will send you a podcast with further advice.

Exercise 12

Decide on your set bedtime at each night and 3 things to do to wind down an hour before bedtime. Eg: Have a bath, make a milky drink, put your pyjamas on ready. Make them a ritual to become a habit.

My bed time will be:
___

My list of bedtime rituals:
___
___
___
___
___
___
___
___
___
___
___
___
___
___

13. Let Rip and Kick the Skeletons Out

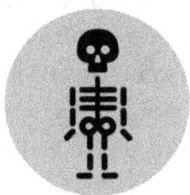

It's never a good idea to bottle things up as they will have to come out eventually. If you feel emotional, angry, frustrated or whatever, go punch the cushions and pillows and have a good shout and swear – just let it out! Believe me, you will feel so much better for it!

Perhaps you have things in your past that need dealing with? These skeletons in the cupboard can hold you back and drain your very soul, so you need to get them out and deal with them. Many of our problems associated with a lack of confidence can be attributed to things that have happened to us in the past – this could be a childhood thing or something fairly recent.

These can be an absolute drain on your future, so you really do need to deal with them. You may need to get expert advice on this, but it will be well worth it to have that emotional freedom.

Have a word with your doctor who can refer you to someone who can help you, or you can source a reputable therapist yourself. If you take this avenue, make sure you check out their credentials – they should belong to a reputable society and have plenty of experience.

It's never too late and so worth it!

Exercise 13

Write down 3 things that have affected you today and decide what you are going to do about them.

14. Take a Risk!

Why not have a go at something completely different like bungee jumping or skydiving? O.K. So those are quite extreme, but you can see where I'm going with this right? Taking a risk and living life on the edge a bit may scare the pants off you, but boy is it a quick confidence booster!

It's never too late to try things out – write yourself a bucket list of all the things you have ever wanted to have a go at. There are women even in later stages of life doing parachute jumps and all sorts of things!

Think back to your younger days when you were full of "I wish I could have a go at that" or try this out for size! We tend to forget about past wishes as life takes over, so sometimes it's good to have a trip down memory lane and dig up the good feelings you had back then; smile at all the silly things you did!

I bet you have at least one memory of a time when you felt really good about something which gave you confidence, so dwell on that and remember how good it felt.

Exercise 14

Write a bucket list and action them one at a time. Remember to tick them off as you complete them!

15. Affirmations

These can be really powerful! Remember, whatever you tell yourself you are conditioning your mind to believe. Tell it something often enough and it will believe it.

My favourite over the last 20 years which saw me through 8 years of university studies as a mature student has been " You can do it", which I think fits just about every situation.

What's yours going to be?

Whatever it is make sure it's positive and repeat it to yourself all the time. Write it down and put it everywhere, on the fridge, on the door, next to the bed, in your cupboards – I wrote mine in every place I would see it so that it was a constant reminder.

Exercise 15

Decide on your mantra and write it below - you may have more than one! Say it/them out loud to yourself at every opportunity.

_____
_____
_____
_____
_____
_____
_____
_____
_____
_____
_____
_____
_____
_____
_____
_____
_____
_____
_____

So, there we are, 15 things for you to take on board to make you feel like a million dollars!

If you've been inspired by this book, then what are you going to do differently starting from tomorrow? Do you want to feel a million dollars again? Let's arrange a time to speak so that I can get to know you and your unique situation. Don't you deserve that?

You can contact me at
https://www.teresabulfordcooper.com/contact

With love,

Teresa. x

About the Author

Teresa Bulford-Cooper is a National & International award-winning Life Coach who specialises in helping Ladies in their second stage of life, to achieve new direction, confidence and self-esteem. She is passionate about seeing Ladies let their inner Goddess out, to be free, happy and enjoy doing what they want to be doing for their next 30+ years!

www.teresabulfordcooper.com
hello@teresabulfordcooper.com
Tel: 01363 775935

www.ingramcontent.com/pod-product-compliance
Lightning Source LLC
Chambersburg PA
CBHW070440010526
44118CB00014B/2121